MY POETIC BLESSINGS

ALL THREE PARTS AS ONE
Copyright 2016

Part I
The Other Side of the Cross
Copyright 2004

Part II
The Other Side of Heaven
Copyright 2013

Part III
The Other Side of Paradise
Copyright 2015

PART I

THE OTHER SIDE OF THE CROSS

THE OTHER SIDE
OF THE CROSS

Poetry By: Michael A. Melice

& The ABC's of How Christians Should Be

The Other Side of The Cross

These poems have come from trials and tribulations in my life. Poetry usually comes from such emotions. The person that has really made poetry come to life is My Lord and Savior, Jesus Christ, from which my title for my first prose book has come from.

I dedicate this book to The Lord Jesus Christ from whom all blessings come forth in this life here on earth, and also from which my Spiritual Blessings in Heavenly places also come. The book of Psalms are in some places poetical in nature. One of my favorite verses in the Psalms is found in Psalm 16:11 which reads from the King James Holy Bible as: "Thou wilt shew me the path of life: in thy presence is fullness of joy; at thy right hand there are pleasures for evermore."

I also want to dedicate this book to the many saints down through the years that have made this life bearable, and to my relatives and friends in Syracuse, New York who stood by me through some of the most difficult times in my life growing up. Psalm 19:14 – "Let the words of my mouth, and the meditation of my heart, be acceptable in thy sight, O LORD, my strength, and my redeemer."

The Title, "The Other Side of the Cross" comes from the fact that we, here on earth today, live in a period of history known as "the dispensation of grace" which is over 2000 years since Jesus Christ hung upon the Cross of Calvary.

"Let the Word of Christ Rule the Meditation of your Heart and Mind each Moment of Time! Your life will become Transformed into a Sweet Melody of Rythme." © 1999 Michael A. Melice

CONTENTS

"Deep In Thought"

©2003 Michael A. Melice

2

God's Unchanging Word

For feelings come and feelings go,
And feelings are deceiving;
My warrant is the Word of God,
Naught else is worth believing.

Though all my heart should feel condemned
For want of some sweet token,
There is One greater than my heart
Whose Word cannot be broken.

I'll trust in God's Unchanging Word
Till soul and body sever;
For, though all things shall pass away,
His Word shall Stand forever.

~ Martin Luther

[The Word of God spoken of here is found only in a King
James Version Bible. I believe these to be the very Words of
God with no errors found within it.]

His Amazing Love

Amazing is His Love,
So faithful and true
But why do I look so blue
You may ask?
The World, the Flesh, the devil without;
But He's given me the Victory within and without.
If it weren't for my Savior's Wonderful Grace,
I could not tell you about the wonderful pace
That He leads me in –
That wonderful Race
That One Day
I will joyfully
Take my position and place
In the Heavens above;
Where His Light will Shine forth
The Brightness of His Love!

~ Michael A. Melice

The Tomorrow
We May Not See

Tomorrow will be soon enough
So many of our assemblies say,
But why put off tomorrow
What one could do Today?!
If only we gave help
To those truly in need
For the words of Christ in their hearts;
So their souls could be freed today!
Yes, we know that we should be doing
This and tomorrow we'll start.
Oh, no, my friend, the Time is Now;
Dear Lord, please touch our hearts:
Because that is where it all starts.

Tomorrows sometimes seldom come
When we put them off today.
So let us ask the Lord above to give us-
Strength to do Tomorrows
Right now Today!

~ Michael A. Melice

"Held By The Artist"
©1982 Michael A. Melice
(Drawn while attending Henninger High School in Syracuse, NY)

Prison Bars

As you gaze upon these prison bars,
Please don't pity me;
For now I am a Child of God,
And I've never been so Free.

We're all bound by prison bars
Locked up behind our sin,
Some, like these, are visible,
But most are Hid within.

There's just one key to Freedom,
No matter where you live,
That key is God's own Precious Son
Who gave all He had to give.

I'm freer now than some of you,
Who roam 'ere where you please.
So don't look in with pity –
Just fall down to your knees.

Ask Jesus for the Key to Life;
Ask Him to Free your Soul;
You'll never know True Freedom,
Until Jesus Christ makes you Whole!
~ Michael A. Melice

John 8:32 – "And ye shall know the truth, and the truth
shall make you free."
[The Source of ABSOLUTE Truth I believe comes from our
Creator, Jesus Christ.]

"Misery and Mo"
©1999 Michael A. Melice
[Bottom drawing by my niece Kala Marie Melice at age 7]

(The verse in the second bubble should be Romans 8:31 KJV.)

One Day At A Time

We may not see the future,
Bright and Bold;
But if we Trust in God,
We can have Peace in doing
What we are Told.

He Promises to Lead us
If we Heed His Plan;
We need not fear
The Unknown, Beast nor Man.

Fear is not of the Lord,
God hath said.
I want Love, Faith and Trust
in it's Stead.

Paul was beaten, stoned,
And nearly killed with a whip;
He knew the most important thing
Was to stay in the Ship.

Oh, sometimes God allows us
To suffer Loss and Pain,
But He always brings Sunshine
After the Rain.

So as we do God's will,
No matter what the Cost;
How much easier Life is to Bear,
When we look at The Cross.

Suffering is what He did
For you and me;
Crucified with Christ
Is where I want to be.

So when I cannot see the Future,
But it looks Painful to be sure;
I can see Calvary's Cross:
His Assurance of Love, Strength,
And Grace for Each Day to Endure...

One Day At A Time!

~ Maria D. Roberts
© 2000 Maria D. Roberts

Critic's Judgement Day

There are, it seems, many ways of life
That few of us express in word to say:
Or create a work of art
That pleases anybody, it seems today!

Today is a far different world
(as when I grew up):
Far more critics, it seems;
You certainly could name a few.
Of those who prefer their vocation or passion~
In words or pain;
Or images of the night
Some say movies, their way;
Or just simply live our life
A totally different way!

So please, don't judge me or pity me
For my Opinion today:
Because I don't enjoy what you may.

Please don't look at me that way.
Simply allow to learn to love me
In my diverse, but different way.

Don't be so narrow-minded
In what you may think
About me or even want to say;

'Cause I don't care
What you may do
To create your life, your way!

Just leave the ONE to judge me:
The Creator, My Savior (all our Sustainer)
To deal with me
From what His Words do say,

I will grant to you an open mind
For you to think what you may want to think,
Only keep it to yourself,
I pray.

Then, and only then, when you create your universe,
Will I obey what you may say;
What you see fit for the human race:
On Judgement Day!

Until that time comes,
Do us all a favor and stop thinking for me:
For where have you ever
Seen a Critic carved in stone
Or given praise for his critical ways!

~ Michael A. Melice

"Redeem the Time Drawn in Your Life"

©2000 Michael A. Melice

If I

If I could go back and undo some wrongs I've done
along the way,
And know that wounds that I have caused were healed
of all the scars today.

If steps I've caused someone to take by thoughtlessness
ways in which I've trod,
Have lead to a confused estate, instead of simple trust in
God.

If someone else still wanders on who followed my
unsteady track,
And lost his way for lack of light because my lantern
globe was black.

If I could gather up and bind the wasted years that I
have spent,
And treat them as they'd never been,
Today I'd be much more content.

I'm pardoned from my undone past- but even so, the
hurt is done,
For out there somewhere in the dark, a soul is lost that I
might have won.

~Author Unknown

Life Today

Another day
House in order
Clean and Inventoried
Bills all paid.

Stretch toward the Sun
Supplements all in one.
Plus water
Some gotta run.
Most love for fun
Redeem your time well.
It won't be here again under the Sun
Save your pennies for a rainy day.

Pay off debt,
Daily chores
No need of a vet,
Vacuum, clean
Discard and throways
UPS is here!
Finally the package has arrived!
Waited so long, it seemed like a year!
Post Office Blues if mail is filled
With wasted paper junk.

Two years ago today,
One of America's Greatest Tragedies changed my world,

Where ever you may be,
Planes unprepared,
The World don't seem to care;
The Government has more Red Tape and foolish
Beauracracy;
Kids in School,
Teachers seem to make their own rules.

Wash and exercise,
In need to eat well and rest.
TV mass media
All cause the audience to scare,
Computers, and terminals
Becoming commonplace here;
Inventions on the rise,
I have one that could be a real big surprise!

Three years here, soon to stare
At the Mirror on the Wall – I see a winner there;
Because of Jesus Christ gave me the hope that all of life
today is looking for here, and everywhere.
So much to do, and time today is few.
Life today is filled with land barren and days gone by.
It's the memory of what used to be that seems to linger
in quiet Altoona Keystone Fair.

~ Michael A. Melice

To My Precious Friend in Christ, Beverly

A friend is a friend you say?
But is a friend a true one of Him?
I have known, Beverly,
Only to see you have been so very kind to me.
When things were rough
And the going was tough,
You were there with most encouraging words.
Your ears were listening,
And words polite,
But most of all you were a helper of this fight.
The battle for the throne
And the Message of Grace
Will always rage on,
But one day you may not be here,
But up there, and no longer will I be able to say
How much you meant to me all those years;
With kind and precious words to encourage me.
Thank you so much
For the day to day prayers
'Cause they'll always be in me to stay.
~ Michael A. Melice

(Poem written for my dear friend, Beverly Pratt in Maine.)
EXTENDING MY PRAYERS AND HIS LOVE AND GRACE
TO YOU AND YOURS,
Brother Michael

2 Timothy 2:3 – "Thou therefore endure hardness, as a good soldier of Jesus Christ."

He Alone

He alone,
Who bore my sins,
Has given to me,
New life within.

The victory I have,
That belongs to you,
And others cannot be seen by the lost!

Oh, how I long to be like
My Savior and Lord;
Who won the battle,
And will, one day soon,
Brings us all home.

'Cause this place we call home
Is not our home
We 'ere roam – just like a battleground.

So we bow to the King, and Lord of Lords,
And count it all joy-
It's when we look to self
That we all plan to fall.

~ Michael A. Melice

Quote by Michael A. Melice
"What people need, they don't want, and what they
want, many times; they don't need!"
© 1999 Michael A. Melice

Poem for Mother

Always so true, unselfish and kind.
Few in this world like my Mother equal to find.
A beautiful life that came to an end,
She died, as she lived: everyone's friend!
The love of my life: here on earth;
a Mother like no other,
You made me who I am-
I love you so much~
You deserve it all!
In Christ's love,
Michael, your son.

~ Michael A. Melice

(Written for my beautiful mother, Angela, who lived in New York.
She died On August 8th, 2011 of Cancer.)

Luke 1:37 – "For with God nothing shall be impossible."

For My Sister, Melissa

To my sister, Melissa
The sweetest dear sister (that a guy could have)
Who could have it all –
Just open up your heart and listen above to Christ:
Who is all in all!
Make Him your man!
Heed these words, sister,
So you wouldn't have to fall!
~Michael. A. Melice

1 Thessalonians 5:18 – "In everything give thanks: for this is the
will of God in Christ Jesus concerning you."
(Written for my sister, Melissa Ann, who resides in New York).

19

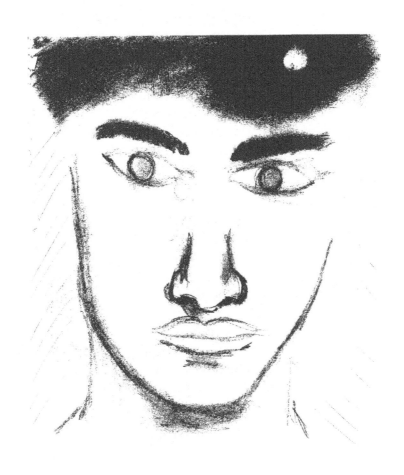

"Thinking of You"
©2002 Michael A. Melice

(The "You" I was thinking of was a woman named Charleen Barber.
She lives in Altoona, PA where we dated briefly.)

20

All in the End

The positive light
I carry to the fight
Is an attitude
Of fortitude needed.
When all else fails
With my ill willed plans
His Word will win
In the end.

The end that we see
Is only temporary –
Till the focus
Of our mind
Never lays hold
Of our past behind us;
But now sees
God's true reality
Of eternal time with Him
As His Glory shall shine forever:
We All will Win!

~ Michael A. Melice

Life Titled

Say yes to life
Continue to be you
In whatever you plan to do
The whole day through;
Know in your heart,
Believe it to be True,
that Christ Jesus is here in me to stay.

So when I get chartered off course,
And get swayed to believe:
That there is somethin' in me that
Only I could do;
That Jesus Christ only wants me to be:

Who I am, not what man can see.
I am sinner, saved by grace:
An example of others to see
What truly the Lord's mercy
Can do for you,
And for me!

~ Michael A. Melice

My Dearest Niece, Marisa

Dear Marisa,
My Niece;
You're sent from above,
You'll always have Uncle Michael's
Guiding Love.
A beautiful smile
That lightens the heart.

So when you're feeling down,
Though were far apart,
Always remember this:
"I will love you, too,
Because Christ Jesus, our Lord,
Gave me to you!"

"Happy First Birthday, Marisa,"
In Jesus Christ's Love,
Godfather and Uncle,
Michael.

~ Michael A. Melice

Written exclusively for Marisa A. Melice
on her very first birthday: February 13th, 2003

"Marisa, Uncle Michael loves you sweetie,
and is praying for you!"

Unsure of Everything?

Often we feel uncertain;
Unsure of most everything.
Afraid to make the wrong decisions,
Dreading what the day may bring.

We keep believing it were possible
To dispel all fear or doubt.
And to figure out in this life
Just what it's all about.

God has given us these answers
Which often times go unheeded.
But if we were to search
His Book of Promises,
We will find what's truly needed
To lift our wayward spirits
And supply us with courage, too.

For with God
Nothing is too impossible
For the Lord our Majesty to do!

~ Michael A. Melice

Just As He Said

He suffered
And Bled –
It was His Blood, He shed
Upon the Cross of Calvary.

He humbled Himself
For me instead
Of Heaven's Glory.

The Cruel Cross
He was Crucified for me;
He died for all my sins on Calvary's tree.

He was Buried –
But the Good News;
Is that He Rose Again:

On the Third Day
Glory to Him,
Just as He Said!

~ Michael A. Melice

The Life We Learn

Principles learned
Life is unturned:
To the Key that Frees
Our Soul to churn.

All that we Inspire,
All that we Attire;
To live our Life
That Path that we might Follow
For Ultimate Freedom.

In our Devices
Never to Forget
The Thing that is Vital.

When it's all over
You better know the Truth
That Soul that we possess
Needs a home in Heaven to rest.
The Paradise that I mention
Is the One from Above.

Whenever we Trust
What the Lord did for us:
Died for our Sins
In our Place on The Cross of Calvary.
He had us in Mind
From Beginning to the End!

~ Michael A. Melice

His Word I Read

The more that I read His Word,
The more I live Above;
The more He tests my Love for Him.

All that I hold dear to my heart
Is to be Conformed such as
My Lord and Savior Jesus Christ had become:
Life from within.

Showing the World that His Word
Is our Will to Win.
All that you can be for Him,
And for thee!

Run the Race
To Achieve
All that you BELIEVE from Him!

~ Michael A. Melice

Trust only Him! Did you gain anything here on Earth: it will all become
Fervent Heat! People are More Important than Things!

2 Corinthians 4:18 – "While we look not at things which are seen, but at the things which are not seen: for the things which
are seen *are* temporal; but the things which are not seen *are* eternal."

"The Mainer From New York"

©1999 Michael A. Melice

28

Heart 2 Hear

(Poem to a friend in Christ, Terri Anyan)

I am His song
Through which He sings
A sweet melody.

With a friend like you
How the world can see:
His joy and grace
With many to grasp the wonder
Of His Sweet Face!

Your care and love toward me
Is a Sweet, Smell of Honesty;
That those around us
I Pray will
One day soon see!

~ Michael A. Melice

This Evil Mind of Mine

Tis evil in the mind
Tainted from the blood of Adam's rib
Deceived from this foolish heart of mine
How low to behold
That sin is a wicked lie!

Dear Father, My God
How I have wasted so much time
On this foolish and wicked world.
I know thy Word to be true
And yet I had drifted so far
From what I knew to be true.

When I read thy Word
And started to pray:
How much in my spirit these words had drifted
So far away;
But thy Word hath rebuked this evil heart of mine,
When it had infiltrated my mind
Not redeeming the time
You have given to me.

Were only a short period in this battle
Found in the mind:
The only way to the light is to renew in my mind,
Thy Word that speaketh right from the wrong thoughts
I had thought a choice to rebel when I realized the time:
Closing on the hourglass of my Life, it is His,
Not mine!

What shall I say in this poem of mine
With not much rhyme:
But I'd chosen the Broad way
Instead of looking the Narrow way
When all of a sudden
The shudder in my soul
Started to propel me and get a hold
Of my trusted King James *
As tears started to roll down –
My Face as I began to pray!

Give me strength in my soul, O Lord,
Thy Word is all I know
To be what I do need:
How I can praise you indeed!

In Thy Precious Word,
The Apostle of our Time
Penned a Wonderful verse that caught my eyes
Of understanding and set my heart
Back to thee:
"...God gave them over to a reprobate mind,
to do those things which are not convenient."
(Romans 1:28b KJV convenient= fitting.)

~ Michael A. Melice

Romans 7:24, 25 – "O wretched that I am! Who shall deliver
me from the body of this death? I thank God through Jesus
Christ our Lord. So then with the mind I myself serve the
law of God; but with the flesh, the law of sin."
*My King James Version Holy Bible

Poem: Untitled

How do I drain the brain
With so much emotional strain
Drug enduced
Veterans loose,
Restless nights,
Heart softened:
Eyes opened wide
How I long to see
The Terrestial skies.

Yet soon bored of no people view
The air sweet and tender;
The air once full of afternoon blue;
Divided by all.
The temporal side soon to be gone
Like the body that grows older.
Young at heart like my Mother's blessed side,
Smiles soon subside
Reality hits all too fast, but true:
Jesus Christ – it seems is the only true one
That can ever Love both me and you equally.
~ Michael A. Melice

Phillipians 4:13 – "I can do all things through Christ which
strengtheneth me."
Phillians 2:13 – " For it is God which worketh in you both to
will and to do of *His* good pleasure."

Bruce:
My Dear Christian Friend

My Tribute to: My Dear Friend, Bruce Rosokoff
To: Wife Jean Rosokoff, son Marty & Gail & family,
Son Carson & Extended Family!

Bruce Rosokoff:
A wonderful Jewish man I once knew;
Oh, we go back aways –
To days when life was much different then;
Those were better days, but that was then.

So here I go with this short little rhyme.
This is for you, dear Bruce, friend of mine;
Because you gave me His Love
And never asked "Why?!"
You always seemed to make time.

This all may not rhyme,
It may seem to all just a few lines.
Here, dear sister
His Wife who seemed to keep right in line
With all that you did, and sometimes even rhymed.
I know that you loved him, and with this said:
I wanted to let you all know
That I Love your family so!!!
~ Michael A. Melice
In His Love and Grace, your Brother and Friend in Christ to
all of you.

Ecclesiastes 3:1, 2a – "To every there is a season, and a time to every
Purpose under the heaven: (2)A time to be born, and a time to die:..."

Happy Birthday Amy

Dear Amy, my friend, the birthday girl,
I pray again and again for many years to come!

Each new day or year we have seen
Should help us to realize
How precious life can be;
Especially those of us
Who know WHO hath brought these things.

For the reason we live and celebrate a year gone by
Is to bring us closer to our Savior, the Lord Jesus Christ.
For He is the Reason WHY we should do everything!

So with these words I bring to thee:
HAPPY BIRTHDAY, DEAR AMY, YOU DESERVE
THE BEST OF ALL THAT CHRIST BRINGS!~

"Why?" you may ask? Because there's something very
WARM about your Heart!

While that poem may not make a lot of sense or rhyme
very well, I just wanted to wish you the VERY BEST
For your 27th Birthday!

Praying for you always, your friend and brother in Christ,
With His Love,
Michael A. Melice

(This poem is written for my friend, Amy Whitfield)

2 Timothy 2:3 – "Thou therefore endure hardness,
as a good soldier of Jesus Christ."

To Cristy, Advice for My Upstate New York Prom Queen

The missing ingredient of this life
Is not now so much what you pray
Or what you have along your pathway;
It is not what you end up with that really creates wealth.

But the Real Success is:
What you CHOOSE NOW to be:
Living for Him and choosing to Win or
Give in to what you choose to fall in.

Sure the World has Riches
And Diamonds too...which drown men in sin;
But the Love from God above;

Far exceeds all that you may want to be or choose to see
Whether here or Italy:
He will always "hear" what you have to say
If you've chosen to Live in Him!
For Jesus Christ is truly the Best Way!

~ Michael A. Melice

(Poem written for Senior Prom Date Cristy Brown from
Henninger Sr. High School in Syracuse, NY. She was by
far the Most Beautiful Woman that evening!)

Phillipians 4:19 – "But my God shall supply all your need
according to his riches in glory by Christ Jesus"

Only Time Will Tell

You think of an era
Of a different kind
When people loved you
As simple as carefree
Only to find that later
We've changed.

Some to the same old beat
While others,
To the same old vein!
That old fashioned thinking
Of using your "brains"
And the world that forgot
To think of history past:
Only to see what will repeat itself again!

But now you're growing older
And life hath become much bolder:
The new wave of living
Hath replaced the old again.

Only now it's becoming what it used to be once more!
Is this the last day
When the trumpet shall call?
Are you going to fall,
Or become more than a conqueror
Since you were known way before Adam was born.
So, finish the race,
With eyes on the prize:
What did you do with
His Word this day;
Did you keep it within
Or store His Word on the floor?

Did you open it up
Or not even peer within?!

The greatest need in our land today:
Is not the answer of how to win the war?!
The answer needed is the answer all around us:
It is written Christ hath once said.
Once for all: He Paid It all!
The "It" was The Cross at Calvary
Most already know...but what do they trust?
It was already paid from Him!
Christ the Lord
Who went to a Cross
His Life He came to die for my sins;
Buried, and rose again on that third day
I just believed it
And can now see it within the Scriptures.
Holy He is,
A message He gave to
The Apostle Paul,
Who gave all that he could.
By inspiration, the Message
Of Grace settled now within me:
My sins are Gone
I am Free to Live FOR HIM.
~ Michael A. Melice

Ecclesiastes 3:8 – "A time of love, and a time to hate; a time of war, and a time of peace."

The Real Battle Within

Where has time taken me this gloomy day?
Nothing but a wretch in this real awful place.
Father, My God, who gave me Life from above;
I sit here and write ashamed and disgraced.
Sin the culprit, self is the motive,
No one to blame, what I have done under grace.
So long ago, light from above –
Gave me much more than just simple Love.
You gave me Your Son,
Who went to the Cross;
Who paid for my sins and
Hung on that cruel Cross.
Buried, and risen again from the dead.
No one believed till He showed Israel His face.
But in His Word with all true grace
He gave us mercy, and peace in it's place.
He did this for you
And He did it for me.
So why do we disappoint Him
When He gives us such liberty?
I know what His Word settled long ago.
If we take and we read it
Each day by the Holy Spirit's control;
Our lives complete in heart and mind of
How we can have true peace and a sound mind.
But listen again of a warning He says,
When a man sows to the flesh,
He will reap corruption instead.

So seek His Word now –
Don't waste your time instead.
Why would you want a cruel life
And possibly be dead?
Dead to sin is what we are in Him,
Living for Christ, living for Him!
Take down self from the throne,
And let the Holy Spirit truly have full control!
Don't give in to the lusts of the flesh:
But fight in the battle to win.
No one ever won by standing aside
And watching the Battle crumble inside.
You're more than a conqueror,
A farmer, too,
A spiritual runner
His race won by farther than the enemy,
A defeated foe knows nothing else
Than fierce flames from his bow.
Putting on Armour,
Armour from God will give you the victory
You don't need to already win.
You see, the battle is on,
The enemy fierce: remember you're still down here.
But you've already got the Victory
though it's feeling like defeat:
That is why His Word is great support from within:
So grin...Why do you frown with philosophical Love
Instead of True Love from Above?
~ Michael A. Melice

Ephesians 5:16 – "Redeeming the time, because the
days are evil."

The ABC's of How Christians Should Be
© 2003 Michael A. Melice

A   Act in a kind, loving way instead of arguing a point you know they may not grasp.

B   Build up someone instead of bragging of your abilities.

C   Climb instead of criticizing differences in others.

D   Dig in The Word instead of depreciating someone who disagrees with your standards of living.

E   Encourage others in their talents and abilities instead of envying what they may do better than you.

F   Fight the Good Fight of Faith instead of fainting under the weight and concerns of the work God hath given you to do.

G   Give the Gospel instead of grumbling about the lost or religious who are blinded to the Absolute Truth for this Dispensation of grace that we live in presently.

H   Help those in Need of your Compassion instead of harming others emotionally with your words and actions.

I   Invite others to your home, church or activity when possible instead of ignoring them.

J   Join the Truth of Life instead of jeering what you do not understand.

K   Kneel in prayer instead of kicking judgement in the face of others who simply have no clue.

L   Love the Lord, yourself and others instead of Lampooning others with words that tear down what God hath created.

M   Move in the area of making a difference instead of trying to mold others to your way of life.

N   Nurture the gift of Salvation and understanding in someone rather than neglecting what he or she does not know doctrinally what you may know.

O   Obey the Word of God and its teaching instead of objecting to what the world is doing.

P   Pray for someone to receive Jesus Christ as Savior rather than pouting about the darkness that causes you misery.

Q   Quality is more important than quantity.

R   Rescue the Truth instead of ridiculing the fools that are negative towards the Words of Truth.

S   Shout the truth instead of shrinking from the intimidation of standing as ambassadors for Christ.

T   Try to be Kind to those who may be offended by you because of your Witness for the Lord.

U   Undergird your loins with the Truth rather than undermining the greatness and power that His Word hath upon your soul.

V   Vindicate instead of Vilifying.

W   Witness with the Gospel instead of wilting from the responsibility.

X   eXamine yourself instead of excusing the sin in your life.

Y   Yield yourself unto God instead of yelling against the "noise" that the World performs.

Z   Zip to do what is right rather than zigzagging to do what is Wrong!

Through Prayer + Studying the Word rightly divided & Obedience = A life of peace and prosperity in the liberty of your mind!!!
Key point in the life of a Christian: Speaking the Truth of
His Word with the love of Christ as prescribed in His Word:
(1 Corinthians 13:4-8a) it says you won't profit nothing.

"Only one Life
Soon will pass –
Only what's done
for Christ Jesus will last."
(old adage, Author Unknown)

Do you want eternal life in Heaven with the Lord Jesus Christ when you die? The answer is simple: Yes or No. If you say yes – Here is the Good News, and it is clear and simple. In order to enter Heaven, you must be perfect.

*The **Bad News** of this problem is that all men are born with a sin nature. A sinner cannot enter Heaven in his sinful state, because God can only accept perfection. The penalty of sin is eternal death and separation from God in a Lake of Fire where that person will experience torment forever.*

*The **Good News** is that Jesus Christ came down to Earth in the form of His own Creation to remove the penalty of sin.*

Jesus Christ Died for our Sins on the Cross at Calvary. He was Buried, and Rose again the Third Day!

*The moment that a sinner believes in his heart (trusts) that Jesus Christ did this work on the Cross for him or her – he or she will receive **ETERNAL LIFE** in Heaven for all **ETERNITY.***

For more information on The Gospel (Good News) and other questions on the Word of God – please visit: www.graceimpact.org

"I Understand"

Hast thou been hungry, child of Mind?
I too, have needed bread;
For forty days I tasted naught
Till by the angels fed
Hast thou been thirsty? On the Cross
I suffered thirst for thee:
I've promised to supply thy need,
My Child, come unto Me.

Perhaps thy way is weary oft,
Thy feet grow tired and lame;
I wearied when I reached the well,
I suffered just the same:
And when I bore the heavy cross
I fainted 'neath the load;
And so I've promised rest to all
Who walk the weary road.

Doth Satan sometimes buffet thee,
And tempt thy soul to sin?
Do faith and hope and love grow weak?
Are doubts and fears within?

Remember I was tempted thrice
By this same foe of thine;
But he could not resist the Word,
Nor conquer pow'r divine.

When thou art sad and tears fall fast
My heart goes out to thee,
For I wept o'er Jerusalem-
The place so dear to me:
And when I came to Lazarus' tomb
I wept- my heart was sore;
I'll comfort thee when thou dost weep,
Till sorrows all are o'er.

Do hearts prove false when thine is true?
I know the bitter dart;
I was betrayed by the one I love –
Who lay close to my heart.
I loved My own, they loved me not,
My heart was lonely, too;
I'll never leave thee, Child of Mine,
My loving Heart is True.

Have courage then, My faithful one,
I suffered all the way,
Thy sensitive and loving heart
I understand today;
Whatever thy grief, whatever thy care
Just bring it unto Me;
Yea, in thy day of trouble, call,
I will deliver me.

~ Susanne C. Umflauf

Prayer of an Unknown Soldier

I asked God for strength, that I might achieve,

I was made weak, that I might learn humbly to obey.

I asked for health, that I might do greater things,

I was given infirmity that I might do better things.

I asked for riches, that I might be happy,

I was given poverty, that I might be wise.

I asked for power, that I might have the praise of men,

I was given weakness, that I might feel the need of God.

I asked for all things, that I might enjoy life,

I was given life, that I might enjoy all things.

I got nothing that I asked for – but everything I had hoped for.

Almost despite myself, my unspoken prayers were answered.

I am among all men, most richly blessed!

[See Phillipians 4:6, 7 KJV}

PART II

THE OTHER
SIDE
OF HEAVEN

The Other Side

Artwork by Danielle Markley, Copyright 2007

# of HEAVEN

by Michael A. Melice

Poetry and Some Artwork

Dedicated to Jesus Christ, My Lord,
My Savior, and to Whom all things are Possible!

TITLE: "Grace Christian Soldier"

I dedicate this book of poetry to My Lord and Savior Jesus Christ from whom this work would have no basis of thought without Him! He is the Word of God manifest in the flesh, Crucified upon the Cross of Calvary having *Died for our Sins, He was buried, and Rose Again the Third Day for all of Mankind. Salvation of one's soul comes to us upon TRUSTING this *Good News in one's Mind. It simply is by Grace Through Faith in this Good News that Secure's a Person's Salvation which God the Father freely gave to us due to the Finished Work of Christ!

I also want to dedicate this book to a wonderful family who once took me in when I moved here to Altoona, PA and have shown to me that "The Other Side of Heaven" can be a good experience despite the trials and tribulations in this life! That family in whom I dedicate this poetry book to also, are Mark, Debbie, Danielle, Valerie, Florine, and Bill (who sadly is no longer with us, but with the Lord in the heavenlies) Markley. The Markley family have in my life here in Altoona, PA shown me what it means to show forth "Grace" to others in this Dispensation of Grace in which we now live!!

*Taken from King James Holy Scriptures, 1 Corinthians 15:1-4

**Dedicated to Jesus Christ, My Lord,
My Savior, and to Whom all things are Possible!**

CONTENTS

I Reflect on Thee

Reflecting on you
Thinking of thee,
Things stand still
My mind can see.

Wondering and waiting
Hoping you'll soon see:
God has made you,
and you for me.

The two of us one
Blinded as one
Together we can see
Apart from each other

Lost as can be...
Just the two of us
Helping each one to see
God has given you,
And you so much for me!

Didn't Think at All

Oh, why'd I run
To just have fun;
Not thinking clearly in my head,
(Oh, the poor thing now seemed dead);
I used my blessed other head-
To think with:
And soon found out
When we don't think at all
That we soon tend to simply fall.
I allowed another to think for me
Cause I "thought" I was having fun:
When actually I was comfortably numb-
And believe you me,
That just ain't no fun!

American Thought

Frustrated and confused
I really hate the "blues".
The Country in trouble,
We know what to do:
Unfortunately those in charge
Continue to lie and abuse.
One day it'll be too late
For all those boys and girls
Whose lives will be ruined;
When elected officials
continue what THEY do:
Only for Them,
not for me and not for you!

This Pain in My Head

There at times
Seems to be
A Yearning
To Begin Again-
And yet it cannot be yet:
Due to this pain
In my head;
My estranged wife
Wants me to be
In Bondage
To her dread.
Making me suffer more:
By Losing Financially!
And just when I think
Things couldn't get worse,
Something new she's done
Only causes me more Pain;
To not only my Pocket
But mostly to my Head!
I gave her simply the Best:
My Time, my Money, my Heart
And my Sweat.
But obviously she's one of
Those Women
Who wants to take all
She can get;
And make me never Forget:
Just a True Idiot
I really had met!!

Copyright 2012 Michael A. Melice

4

Borrowed Time

Turning inward
Thoughts appear
Looking out my
Window Blind.
Have this Day
I've used to surrender my Mind, and
Redeeming the Time:
His Will Divine,
Or have I waned
Another Day
Of Useless activities
That bring Glory
To my Desires.
All the More
My thoughts I hear
In the Backdrop
Of Crowded Time
I Chose His Day to use
On empty Desires;
That bring no Glory
To the Lord Divine:
Who Deserves all the Glory
From Everlasting time to Everlasting Time,
In every Direction of Eternal Time.

He has always

Been in what we call 'Time'...

Because He is without Time in His Eternal Mind

That Always was, way before Time.

Do we begin our Day

Thinking this Way?

Or have we Become

Useless with our Time.

That He gives us

Each Day

That frankly is Borrowed Time

From the Father of Glory Divine;

Who will Show whose Time has come

When all the Universe

Will see Christ Come:

And once Again Step onto the Earth

He Previously Designed!

Poem for Mother

This Poem is written
For my Mother,
God Bless her;
For now her home is above
In Heaven with the One I love:
Jesus Christ My Lord.
He, who gave me such
A Wonderful mother:
Whose energy and drive
I believe I've inherited
Have helped pull me through;
The difficult pathways
I've trodden on below here.
Due my own bad decisions
I've made myself.

It's because of my Mother
That I've been able
To work hard, and love others.
You see, my Mother
Was like no other: an other-people person
That coincides with our
Lord above who
Wants us to be~loving others

Despite what they may be,
Do or say;
For Christ Jesus our Lord
Had died for you and me,
And has given us the power
To forgive others because
He did this for us~so we could all be:

Living in heaven above
And one day we shall all see
My Beautiful Mother
Who I believe happens to be~
Now with the Lord, and
Of course so many other's!

Some Quotes of Mine

"Patience is the key to Joy!"
"Sorrow of parting with Loved ones now
will one day forever bring true happiness."
Copyright 2008 Michael A. Melice

"One of the Greatest joys a Man can possess
is making a woman happy in this life!"
Copyright 2013 Michael A. Melice

"To Learn something- you've got to Read it."
"To Know something- you've got to Write it."
"To Master something- you've got to Teach it."
Copyright 2012 Michael A. Melice

"Let the Word of Christ Rule the Meditation of your Heart and
Mind each Moment of Time! Your Life will become Transformed
Into a Sweet Melody of Rhyme!"
Copyright 2003 Michael A. Melice

"The closer you get to the ground,
the closer gravity takes you down!"
Copyright 2003 October Michael A. Melice

Future, Bleak!

Dark and lonely
All alone
Not really feeling
At home:
In this life
I call my own.
Feelin' Blue,
Feelin' Bleak
It's only 'cause
The future looks bleak!
Bleak I tell you,
It's not my thought
But indicators
In headline news;
What a waste:
To think our great country
Once had it all!
Please don't despair
Christendom says:
It's soon to be
Our Lord at last,
And that was written
Long ago in the past!

My Once Friend Gordon

Feelin' low
Feelin' blue,
It's only cause, Gordon:
I was thinkin of you!
You, my dear friend
Now gone far away,
Never to hear your humorous voice say;
"Hey, How do you do?"
Missing you each and every day
Just glad your not suffering,
Down or feelin' blue.
Now your up with
Our Savior and Lord Jesus Christ.
Oh, how much I think daily of you~!
We all do, the family of God
Through our hurt and pain,
We know that your smiling
Even when we have Rain!

Copyright 2011 Michael A. Melice

Once Upon a Dream

Once upon a time
This dream of mine
I saw the two of us
Together, it seemed
Such a beautiful rhyme.

We chose to be one
As the Lord God had
Made us two both one.

There upon my bed
I knelt down instead:
To close my eyes
And pray...

This my dream
I'd like one day
To sing...this dream
I long to see
Just one blessed woman for me.

This, O Dear Lord
Is all I want for me.
Riches, and things
Fancy clothes
And huge diamond rings:
That's not
Something I need.

Just one beautiful soul
Who would love and make me whole.
She would appreciate the beauty you, Lord, can see.

In her I would possess
The joy of give and take
Her warm, genuine, confident embrace.
This young girl now old
Her soft sweet hands
Would bring my soul to thee:
O Lord – it would really be
A dream that becomes a beautiful reality!

It Happened

And so it happened
And all else failed
Until the truth denied
Was beyond the stream.

The stream of tears
Running down my face
It all seemed like another day;
Here we go again today.

Until I realized
The choice I made
Was far away from the one I should choose,
Cause choices bring to us:
Where life happens to be.

A road, a path, a circle of grace
Never getting there
Only failing here
Until you stop choosing
The path of lies.

And only then can you erase
The web of lies
You've piled so high
And then it tumbles
And then it fails . . .

To where you began
A year gone by?
Two years it's been
And but grace

Lights you the way
Of yesterdays. . .
Yesterdays and all you know
Go totally right out your door
And there you stand
Where all else fails

Upon the truth
Not any tale
But the one who
Gave His Grace

That puts a smile
On every child,
On every face.

It remains here that
I tell you this story
Due to the grace
He has bestowed on us all
That God has given to man
Because Christ the Son
Paid with His Blood
For the entire Human Race!

And so we all stand
Because of His Grace,
That I can tell you
His life has been passed
Onto you and me both.
That only by Faith
We can Stand
Upon Earth in
His High and Holy Place.

Simply a Vessel
For His Mercy
Has shown Mankind
The Beauty of His Grace
Which leads us to the Truth
Where His Word
Has shown the World
Just how man's disgrace
Turns out to be God's
Greatest Triumph
In the entire Human Race!

Deep in Thought

Alone, and at home
I began to think of life:
Here today, gone tomorrow.
Seems like it drifts faster
than one thinks.
Before we all know it
middle age has come to us
and your life is not
what it seemed it would be.
Because from what I do know
Scripture tells of man's fall
in the Garden of Eden
where Adam fell and
the rest of mankind affected.
To create a life that is never
as you might like it to be.
Realizing the imperfect world
in which we live,
and all of us imperfect beings...
Our lives sometimes
become what we never
thought they would be:
Imperfect, and apparent
that as Adam sinned
So we begin again:
in a circle of life
that never will be
Perfect as the Lord God
who had first created us to be;
but chaotic vast and vague
in a world that never rests
till once again
God will make perfect
what man has made one big mess!

Copyright 2012 Michael A. Melice

Time in a Dream

Time like a river
Travels downstream,
Waiting to relinquish
All control of my dream.

Dreams turn to time
Time opens wide,
The billowing sorrow
Now closing this rhyme.

Wide opening of my eyes
Love opens my blinds,
My true woman sighs
At my face as it shines.

True love I have found
This has to be true,
Stop feeling blue
Because she loves you too!

Wow, I think
Nothing now stinks,
It's all smelling like roses
How Love leaves you blinded.

Then like a fast river
I open my eyes,
Only to see that it was all in my dream:
Now just a lie, caught in my mind;
To make sense of my reality
Of longing to be asleep again!

Copyright 2012 Michael A. Melice

Poem for Today

I lived
And loved thee
To let others "see":
The fellowship of the mystery.

It was all
His work through me
A vessel,
Fit and set apart
For Jesus Christ to receive all the glory!

Just a light
Is all I want to be;
In all that I do
With a renewed mind continually.
Consistently is what
I strive for to say to thee;
"Not my will be done,
But thine let be;"
Never enough time I believe
To redeem
In these "last days of mine",
To be used for thine honor,
and exceeding great Glory!

Living in Him

Like Life I cast myself
Into the water of living
And there I looked upon
The dead and the living.

Living you see with eyes open wide
Dead who aren't living eyes open shut.
More I came to realize
That Life is only living...

For Him it's beyond what
Your eyes can see.
Believing His Words
And Allowing the Truth:

To Open your Mind
To what is Real,
And what isn't.

Soon I discovered
The secret of life:
It's not my own
To Use or Disown.

It's His Life within me
Trying to perceive me;
And allow Him to live:
Within my Mind I can see!

Copyright 2013 Michael A. Melice

Where I Belong

One day I'm coming
Coming back home.
Home's where I belong
Created by the One
The One who Died for me;
And gave me His Life:
A Life so abundantly.

If I choose to live
Like where I come from
I'd never look back:
But press onward.

Oh, if you love your Life
To Honor Him,
You'd lose your Life
And take on His!

The Beginning of My Day

As way leads on to way
I stepped across the day
To find my early dawn.
Yet another day,
It was there that I lay
Upon my bed to pray,
And Thank the Lord for His New Day!

It was there in my own manifest mind
That I lay there thinking of another day,
Hopefully kinder...
They called for rain today,
And yet knowing another kind of weather
Lay hold of just outside my windowpane.

Hoping to find yet another day
There upon my bed came the image
To speak my mind:
To the Lord Above,
My Christ, My Love
Was simply to ask for a good
And kindhearted day of rhyme;
To speak the truth to others
To obey His Word
Yet another day of mine!

Copyright 2012 Michael A. Melice

What Used to Be

A memory
A reflection
What used to be
Now gone like the wind.

As I sit here I think
Contemplating
Life past...
Gone now
Is time,
Youth no longer on my side.

The world
Turned round,
Upside down.
All around me
The only thing left
In the world to see:
Is God's Holy Word;
Absolute Truth
To make sense
Of you, and of me.

Other than that
Man really can't see
The beauty of creation.
We CAN see...
How when truly viewed upon
Has destroyed God's World
All of us sadly can see!~

Time for Change

Time to change
No longer time to waste.
Those who want to know me
Will reach out and call or write me:
People that don't think they're above me.

God Almighty made me very special
To reach out to others who need me,
But those who choose to ignore me
Obviously don't really love me.

If you care about someone
You will reach them 'cause you care:
But those who choose not to
Have shown what you mean to them.

So, forget the self pity
And move on with your life:
One Life He gave to us
One Life to show your Real Love
For all that Christ did for us
To reach out and love us,
Should embolden us;
To Change our Lives for Him
And not dwell on sin, but dwell on Him.

His Word that can
Transform us,
To manifest His Wisdom
And show the World
What God can do for you
And what He has done for me!

Copyright 2013 Michael A. Melice

I Wait for You!

In my Heart of Hearts
I wait for you...
Wondering, waiting
Praying you will be true.

Believing you're out there.
True to your words,
True to your heart
True in your mind,
Where should I start?

I will start with your hair
Straight as can be, but
Curly or wavy is fine by me.
I will come to your eyes.

With Beauty I see
Whether brown, or blue
Green or hazel too:
They are eyes for me...
Eyes that can see,

When I am near
Eyes that tear,
When I'm far from thee.
Eyes that don't wander,
Easy for me;
Eyes that envelop
A world that you see:
With myself in it
You're happy I can see.

A mouth that I love
To kiss every night
A mouth with such words
That carry us into the night.

A mouth for such love
You express only to me.
A mouth overflowing
With lovely words
I am hearing.

You nose always knows
The smell of me.
A nose that can enjoy
A good meal from me.

Your ears have a beauty
That can hear words I speak;
Only to you words that I think:
Will tell you how much I love you!
A sound of peaceful beauty
To tell you what I think!

I wait for you, dear lady,
I wait all the day long.
Believing and wondering
How life will bring you
To me, a man that is genuine
for all the world to see!

My Cousin Roberta

She was beautiful and caring
A soul like no other
She gave three children
a home to call their own.

She was a favorite cousin of mine
due to her love and grace;
Who will shine in my mind
of fond memories I have of her.

Always taking the time to spend
with her because of the beautiful way
she had with words and care:
She gave to all who knew her!

Missing you, Roberta;
yet knowing one day we will
see each other in heaven
where you now live and call home!

*Note: Written for Cousin Roberta (Ferko) Ayres who
lived in Phoenixville, PA*

This I Know

I do not know what next may come
Across my pilgrim way,
I do not know tomorrow's road
Nor see beyond today.
But This I Know- My Savior knows
The path I cannot see,
And I can trust His Wounded hand
To guide and care for me.

I do not know what may befall
Of sunshine and of rain.
I do know what may be mine
Of pleasure or of pain.
But This I Know- My Savior knows
And whatsoever it be,
Still I can trust His Love to allow
What will be best for me.

In Him shall all my spiritual needs be met
I can trust His Love for me:
Who has not failed me yet!

Article: Peace Within

The Greatest fear I believe for man is to have peace in knowing that one day he will be free. Free from the stink of Humanity in his natural form. The Pollution, and Depression, The Evil and Corruption; Political Psychobabble; Television Talk Shows; Bad food; Streetlights and Bad Weather. The Taxation; Fraud; Blue and White Collar Crime; Rape and Assault; Survival in a Foreign land.

America: the Greatest Experiment in the History of the World for Freedom. Have we advanced? How free are we really?

I was talking to a friend of mine one night about how much freedom we have in America. As we began to talk: I sensed that we may not necessarily have more freedom; but different freedom from the rest of the planet. The Third World countries have poverty and Depression. Europe may have more sophistication and advancements in medical science. As for the other countries they only wish they lived in America. The poorest of the poor here are rich compared to the majority of those in poor countries.

Are you truly Free? The only place for any man's freedom: in his Mind. All of us have some obligation in the slightest that keep us in bondage to something or someone.

Freedom is what you think it is, and the Holy Scriptures make it clear that the truth will MAKE you free!

Have you ever known the truth to do this in your life? Of course you have no doubt. When I graduated from High School; having known the truth and been tested in 4 years I became free from the rigors of that part of my life.

When I trusted Jesus Christ for what He did for me at the Cross of Calvary I received Eternal Salvation for my soul. I had become free in knowing where my soul was going. My soul would one day belong with Jesus Christ in the 2nd Heavens.

Freedom is all a matter of perception. The majority of people ever born in this world don't perceive this truth. I believe that even when you are freed from this thought in your mind, You still truly aren't free! You pay Taxes; Bills; Clean; Cook; Drive a Car; Talk on the phone, etc...Work never ends!

I used to hear people say 'Free and in love'. Oh, really?! Love still takes work to last. It is liberating in the entire sense of the word "free"; but it won't last long unless you WORK at making it last.

So, when you lay down your head tonight on your pillow thanking God for your freedom, know this much: Your free in this life only in your mind when you have the absolute truth to acknowledge that He one day will set you truly free from the trials of life. Joy is definitely a part of life; but real Joy will be known only in the realm of your Home in Heaven where there is no Sorrow or Pain.

In Much Wisdom is great sorrow, and in much knowledge is Much Grief; but in Heaven there is freedom from the mortality we have on this Earth. Earth is the Center of where reality is only Temporal, but Eternity is where there is eternal joy and Peace apart from the sufferings of this present time. Time which cannot be compared to perfection in Christ Jesus with Him where Time does not exist.

The Question then remains for you: "Do you have Peace within yourself?"

Shakespeare once wrote, "To be or not to be. Is that not the Question?"

Well, you can be free or you can choose not to be free; which will it be depends on what you Believe----in your Mind!

Life is what you think it to be. You have Food, Water, Clothing, a Car, Shelter and those who Love you; Yet most of us choose to think,

"Woe is me, I wanna be free." You can be free if you think just like me...You're free to choose. One of the Creator's Greatest Gifts to Mankind. To believe or not to believe: Freedom, and peace within to choose to be whoever and whatever you want to be! Question Again Remains,

"Whatcha gonna do when the Coroner Comes for you?" I plan to enjoy knowing in my mind that one day at my Funeral I will be with my Creator, Savior and Lord Jesus Christ.

It was the reason He came here, and the He is the reason I live, and you live!

Will you live knowing, or die wondering? If you could Know Absolutely 100% that your Soul was going to be in Heaven or Hell: wouldn't you choose Heaven over Hell? That, my friends is as most would say, "Uh, that's a no-brainer." Which means, you don't even need to think about that!

A Prophet of Israel once said, "There is no peace to the wicked." That very same Prophet said, "Thou wilt keep him in perfect peace, whose mind is stayed on thee: because he trusteth in thee."

When you Trust the very one who Created you: You have Peace because your mind is stayed on His Truth. The Truth won't set you free; it will make you free. Your choice to believe it will set you free in this life.

"Every Story has an ending as does life, but the end of life is simply a beginning to the Afterlife. Will you spend Eternity in Heaven or Hell in the Afterlife? The Choice is yours?!~"

Copyright 2013 Michael A. Melice

RESURRECTION POWER

How comes this flower to bloom so fair,
　　With loveliest fragrance to fill the air?
A short time ago the seed lay dead,
　　The cold, wintry ground its desolate bed.

But now, behold from the dampened earth,
　　Without a sound to betray its birth,
This thing of beauty has blossomed and grown
　　To possess a loveliness all its own.

And as we view it, standing there
　　With a majesty quite beyond compare,
A mighty conviction gains the heart:
　　This beautiful flow'r has a counterpart.

Our Savior once suffered and died for sin.
　　Though no one so righteous as He had been.
It seemed that the devil had sealed His doom
　　As they buried His body in Joseph's tomb.

But what is this wonder that greets our eyes
　　As the rays of the third morning's sun arise?
Behold, He is risen! The grave could not hold
　　The Author of Life, the Anointed of God!

And now the dead who have trusted His name,
　　Though sleeping in Jesus, will rise again
With bodies more glorious, than this flower
　　-Sown in weakness, but raised in power!

-Cornelius R. Stam

Given permission by publisher, Berean Bible Society
(C.R. Stam passed away years ago)

31

PART III

THE OTHER
SIDE
OF PARADISE

The Other Side

Artwork by Michael A. Melice, Copyright 2013

# of PARADISE

by Michael A. Melice

Poetry and Some Artwork
Dedicated to Jesus Christ, My Lord,
My Savior, and to Whom all things are Possible!

Copyright 2015
Michael A. Melice

Dedication

I dedicate this Poetry Book First and Foremost to my Lord and Savior Jesus Christ from which all things were created, sustained, and given Everlasting Life with Him for those who Believe! I dedicate this Poetry book also to all those who make other's see "The Fellowship of the Mystery" and never give up showing all others The Gospel of Jesus Christ according to the Revelation of the Mystery! (Ephesians 3:9; Romans 16:25KJV).

Also, I want to make a Special Dedication and Memorial to My Wonderful Mother, Angela Marie (Donatis) Manzi who never gave up on loving me, her Family, her Friends and Strangers. She gave to me her Wonderful Personality and Determination in doing what gives me Purpose in Life: Uncovering the Truth, and Telling Others!!

My nephew Dana, and great nephews Vincent and Javiean

CONTENTS

v

The Way

He is the Way
Not the Broadway;
not the Wrong Way,
but the Right Way!

Not my Way?!
But His Way...
For He is the Truth
His Word,
Is the Light, that, too, we hide.

He, Jesus Christ
is the Ever, Burning Light
in a Sin Cursed World:
Where many Fight
Him all the Way!

We need to give
It all to Him,
and Say;
Dear Lord
Help me
to Live
My Life
Your Way, not Mine!

Valentine Day Poem

God didn't promise days without pain,
Laughter without sorrow,
Sun without the Rain;
But He did Promise Strength for the Day,
Comfort for the Tears
And Light to find His Way!
Happy Valentine's Day to All!!

Copyright 2008 Michael A. Melice

The Truth

Some Get it.
Some Got it.
Some Flaunt it,
Some Want it!
Some Know it
Some Show it,
Sadly, most of us will blow it!!

Copyright 2014 Michael A. Melice

His Will, Not Mine

Trusting in Him
Here by my side
The World on its own
No "Matter" inside;
True to His Word
Transforms your Inside
Change is for Him,
Your Glory to Hide.

You're not on your Own
He's still on the Throne!
Recall to your Heart
Your Prayer will start:
Change from within
His Glory I shout!
Is not for My Will,
But His fruit my Win.
With Christ Jesus we all win:
If we follow His Will, and not our Own!

Copyright 2006 Michael A. Melice

A Poemette

We mutter and sputter,
We mumble and grumble
Our Feelings get hurt
We can't understand things;
Our Vision grows dim,
When all we need is, Simply:
A Moment with Him!

Our Real Home

Heads are turned
Lives Unlearned,
We Fail to see
The Difference.

When all else fails
We look to self
Instead of Christ;
Who gave His Life
For our Eternal Home.

In the Heavens, Far Above!

Remember

Remember the days
When you were
Young,
And now life's gone
by...
And it use to be Fun
to watch
All the women;
And then you were stung?
By the woman you thought
Was the very one?
But it turned out,
As the old saying goes,
"Girls just wanna have Fun!"

Amazing Love

Amazing is His Beautiful Love
He gave to me
If only others could Rightly see;
That my Lord and Savior
Jesus Christ, did die for me.

The Cruel Cross at Calvary
Had taken away my Sins;
I was Buried, and Rose
Again with Him.

The Moment I take
My eyes off Him;
And Look to the Circumstances
Of my Life,
and not give them
To Him:
I fall to pieces
As those who don't know Him.

But the Greatest News
Is this my Friend,
That I've got
the Victory already - and
It is sealed, altogether, within!

Copyright 1999 Michael A. Melice

6

Fireman's Prayer

When I'm called to duty, God,
wherever flames may rage.
Give me strength to save a life,
whatever be its age.

Help me to embrace a little child
before it is too late,
Or save an older person from
the horror of its fate.

Enable me to be alert to
hear the weakest shout.
And quickly and efficiently
to put the fire out.

I want to fill my calling
and give the best in me,
To guard my every neighbor and
protect their property.

And if according to your will,
I have to lose my life,
Please Bless with your Protecting hand
my Children and my Wife.

Author Unknown

This Lonely Life

Fools fall in love...
Who don't know?
Here I stand in awe
Of your Abounding Grace.
You have given to me.
Praying for Others
To see your Character of Face.

Alone in my room
Misunderstood by others
Who really need your Mercy and your Grace.
But you, O Lord
I love all the more,
'Cause I know
That you alone
Have given me the Faith.

The Faith
to Please Thee
Is what you've provided:
By the Blood
Of your Precious Son
Who became my sin.

He was spit upon,
Mocked at
All in Disgrace.
He did it willingly,
Because He knew
Who was in Control.
He loved His Father
And only wanted to do His will;
that my friend, is my Ultimate Goal!

By feasting on His Word and prayer,
Not all alone,
But I want to see others
Not merely on the phone.

There are a faithful few
In this State
Who love to hear
His Word above all else.

And not just Blame
Others for their sin,
But simply tell it:
All to Him!

TITLE: "Three and a Half Year Rough Road"

THE PICTURE I DREW HERE
IS SYMBOLIC OF A 3½ YEAR
PERIOD OF MY LIFE THAT
WAS A VERY ROUGH ROAD.
THE WOMAN SYMBOLIZES
WHO I FELT I NEEDED
TO RESCUE ME (HENCE
HER BEING ON A HORSE)
THE YELLOW LIGHT IS
SYMBOLIC OF THE
TRUTH.

Copyright 2012 Michael A. Melice

10

His Love

The Love in His Heart that
He arose from the Grave
Has put a New Song
In My Life long ago.

The Living Word
He gave to the Apostle Paul -
Never to Depart.

In You, Loved one
A Friend the Lord gave:
Thou miles apart;
This Amazing Love
The Lord Savior Gave
You and me.

His Love for us
At the Cross of Calvary,
The Road of Suffering
He Freely Paid,

So others can know
Of the Wonderful Hope
that Awaits them:
By Faith in Him!

His Amazing Love He Gave

Amazing is your Love
Abounding in Mercy,
And True Grace.
I look toward thee,
O Lord, and Thank you
for the Goodness
Of this place:
You gave to me
Where ever I may be...
Cause true Contentment
Is Fulfillment in,
My Daily Food
Of Thy Word;
Clothed in True Righteousness!

Copyright 2000 Michael A. Melice

Untitled Love

Father, you gave to me
Your Son, Christ Jesus,
Who hung on a tree
Called The Cross of Calvary.

It was there that you showed
The World and me
True Love and True Mercy.
You've suffered long
And gave still
More Grace to me.

I know even when
I'm not sowing
To the Spirit:
You pick me up there,
And there your Grace
Abounds even more:
I've so much to be Thankful for
Because I'm so Grateful for your Neverending Love!!

Copyright 1999 Michael A. Melice

In It All

It's not in seeking
It's in Serving.
It's not in Getting
It's in Giving.
It's not found in this world;
It's Found in Christ Jesus who made it all!

Let Life Come Out

The Light within!
But the true life
That we keep inside
Needs to come out
To tell others about;
Because others
Need to see,
To believe they walk by sight,
And not by Faith, and
Don't get the reason why
we are here:
It's to serve Thee, O Lord-
The One
Who placed us all here!

What's Life All About?

Round and round
The Earth goes,
When it stops only God knows.

We look all around
At what we have done;
Everything we've done
Makes no sense, but maybe
A whole lotta fun?!

Unless we look to The Book,
God's own Precious Word
About God's Holy Son.
For his Holy Words
Show us the Only Way,
The truth it explains;
The Light opens our eyes
To things we need know~!

When all is said and done
Only what's done for Christ
We'll Behold and will be Told;

Of which His Life
Truly Becomes our own
Under God the Holy One!
Jesus Christ the Lord,
The Savior, The Son:

Who Will Rule and Reign
His Kingdom Here on Earth
And Also in the Heavenlies!

This Moment in Time

The Moment is Mine
How Life can Change
In a split second rhyme
that now seems true;
What does it mean, and
What can we do?

The Transformed Mind
Can Expand beyond me, Expand beyond you...
It can take what we Think
And Become what we Dream.

From the first thought to the last
it can make your life Better
It can make your life Beautiful
It can make your time here:
Break free from me... break free from you,
Boxed square nothing there...
And be something for all to see.
More importantly, this Moment in time
was made by the One
We fail to call the Son
Who gave us His life
and Shed His Blood
so you could read
All about Him as God the Son,
The Everlasting One!

Nobody at Home

Rushing here
Rushing there,
But you'll never find
many families
in one spot
for very long.

Calling here
Calling there:
Never anyone
at home anymore.

Isn't it any wonder
America has fallen apart?
With Father and Mother
Not at home, and
Children no where
to be found;

Is it a wonder
Families even have a home -
when they're
never around?

Here I stand
All by myself,
All alone.

Just me at home
Can't reach
anyone ever
much by the phone.

Looking and
Searching,
On a big computer screen:
Trying to connect,
Hoping to find
Someone to reach
Yet unable to see;

The way Society
has come anywhere to be;
Digital words,
Spoken not heard.

Viewed and seen
Through this great machine:
The world has called Home;
My, my, what a sad, Tragedy we have become.

Do you Truly Love?

The more I love them,
The less I am loved.

Some turn away
Some turn within,
Some really don't care:
So why don't I give in?

Because of His Word...
I live to give
Thy truth for all
to hear and to see!!

What Happened, America?

Home you say-
The Red, the White, and the Blue.
America
gone totally downhill...
This land
I walk on:
is not my True Home.
As I ere roam-
no ties
to this earth;
that I'd miss down here-

cause My True Home
is way high, up there.

Further than the stars
that we can see.
More than mere man
has ever given to me.

It was my Savior,
the Lord Jesus Christ
who gave His Life
for me: that He
would die, just for you, and for me.
This is the eye of faith
That I use to see.

I'm not some
loon or nuts
as others have
had their say about me;
but a soldier that The One
who gave
his Blood,
and Life
so you and I
could have true liberty
in this country now turned:
Commie ... and that ain't for me!
I am an American
with still Some Liberties
Not too plain to see.

If Others Could See

The Lord above
is here Below
He Lives in me,
and gave to me:
the Victory!

No Matter the struggle,
pain or fight:
through his Word and Prayer...
I will not despair.

Because He gave
to Me "the Mystery"
never before revealed
to any other,
but the Apostle Paul
first to see.

If only Others
could see it all:
the Confusion, and the Division
in the Church today
would be: All so small...
One wonders, sometimes at all!

TITLE: "Nancy and Family"

Nancy, daughter Johnna, and great niece Francesca

Copyright 2015 Michael A. Melice

Rhythm in Rhyme

As you listen to the sound of your heart,
Remember not to stumble upon the line.
The line to know the lie from the truth
A truth known only in time:
that revealing all that our Father
Has planned, on doing, is found
In the Words of His Book we know
as the Word of God, the King James Holy Bible.

When you realize that this life
is seemingly like a dream;
when you get near the end
of a vapor that led you here:
To Read that He Gave His Son's
Only life for you and me:

He Died for Your Sins and Mine, was buried
and Rose again the Third Day.
Now you know that what He said
He will give to you, His Life, and not your own.

For living this life in Christ
Will Transform your Mind; and in time
You will Become a Sweet Melody of Rhyme!

Copyright 2013 Michael A. Melice

For Upton Plessinger

Upton, Upton - now that your gone;
Though I've not known you very long
So few times we've spoken:
but this one thing
I know tis true...
you're with Christ Jesus
and there One Day
I will meet again with you!
Alas, no doubt,
many in The Body
are fallin' out o'time,
it seemeth before too long-
We will All hear the Shout
When the Lord from Heaven:
Will surely Take us Out!

<u>*Some Quotes of Mine*</u>

"Man takes a Kiss, Kiss takes a Kiss,
then the Kiss takes the Man!

Copyright April 2014 Michael A. Melice

"Spiritual Life that is Healthy Produces
Good Physical Health."

Copyright 1999 Michael A. Melice

"It was Faith that Saved me;
it was Faith that secures me, and it was Faith
that will get me through this
Journey of Life I do not always Understand."

Copyright 1999 Michael A. Melice

Jesus Christ Freed Me

Jesus Christ is
the Winner you see.
He paid the ultimate
Price So I could
be set Free!
It's not Simple
or Quick, but
the Change
He makes
is the one
that will Free
your Soul to Be;
Who all you Need to be!
He Gave my Life
Purpose, and Meaning.
And yes, this is true,
It could surely happen to you;
If only you would
Take that First
Step of Faith:
For you will Rejoice
For all Eternity
that you did this Day!

Copyright 1999 Michael A. Melice

My Life - Your All

My Lord,
A Consuming Fire.
Have you placed yourself
on the Altar today?
Have you Given it all
to Him?
Hear what I say -
You are His;
You're not your Own,
do you really know
The Price He paid to own?
His own Life
He brought to Earth
Have you given Him Full Control?
Here I stand
O Lord, I pray-
Take my All
And Let me not Stray,
Nor falter or fail
to do His will,
Cause I am yours
Each Day still.
You Besought me
To Present myself-
A Living Sacrifice this day-
Renewed in your Word;

Not selfish or cruel
to Enjoy His life
and allowing "The Hold"
that you have placed on me-
To Call me your very own
With your Seal, Never to Appeal.
Not my Will,
But I give My all -
Produce the Fruit in me:
Whatever the Condition, Place
or Situation-
Allow me to live
in the Highest Calling;
Serving Thee
not for Gain to me,
but because of your Love and Mercy
you Gave to me.
A Free Will Offering of Thy Blessed Son-
To give what is Yours
Back to Thee, from Before "The Fall";
in the Garden of Eden
Where Adam, the first man, truly had it All!!

Copyright 25 July 2000 Michael A. Melice

The World Fell Apart

Here we stand
a Nation in Crisis
as we watch our Land
Slowly disintegrate~!

Terrorism on our Airplanes
War overseas,
Why Isn't America NOW
What it ought to be?

Nation against Nation
Child against Parent
Sounds like Morals
Have really gone Askew!

The World has
Schemed and Plotted
Something not so very New.
A Seabed of sin
A Wicked game;
Which is why
Hell was created:
But not Prepared for me and you!

With peace in your heart
And Joy and Love
in Heaven Above,
Though Temporal
This Life seems to be;
God will one day
Make it all New,
Every last part!

A Tale Man has Seen

From whom this life begins
to weave a Tale of Man
can spin of Truth indeed.
Which Man has lied
to Tell sweet Love
Only Christ Abide.
Upon the Cruel Cross
Man's real fate.
Through Christ the Lord
Upon He gave
His Life, His Love
To man doth hide,
The Truth we know
Within His Word of God
Whose Christ gave all
Whose Life Gave Birth.

A Birth Renewed
Who Believe of Christ
Who Died for us;
We choose to hurt.

Israel

Oh Israel, I have seen your hills,
     and, Jerusalem, where the Spirit fills,
My heart each time I visit there,
     with love and hope I need to share,

And many in this world I know,
     have not felt what it's like to go,
Our footpaths where our Jesus went –
     Our Savior, the one the Father sent.

He lived and died, then rose – our Lord –
     to thus fulfill the Holy Word;
It says He would give it all for us –
     forgive our sins, teach us to trust,
And direct us each and every day,
     making us eager to live His way.

I want to go again and feel,
     the atmosphere that is so real,
So Holy in that land of old
     where the greatest story ever told,
was lived by a very special man,
     Jesus, who roamed those hills, that land,
And showed that we must love all others,
     make our neighbors our sisters, our brothers.

We thank you Lord that we have your love,
     to bless, protect, guide from above.
And when it's all been said and done,
     the love of God and the Holy One
Will comfort us, fill every need,
     and be with us for eternity.

Written by Tom Orlando in 1996 after a trip to Israel
Copyright 1996 Tom Orlando

NOTES

Made in the USA
Middletown, DE
12 May 2023

29862653R00076